Instant HubSpot Dashboard Customization

Customize your HubSpot dashboard to generate
qualified inbound leads for your business

Deepan Siddhu Nagarajan

BIRMINGHAM - MUMBAI

Instant HubSpot Dashboard Customization

First published: January 2014

Production Reference: 1230114

Published by Packt Publishing Ltd.
Livery Place
35 Livery Street
Birmingham B3 2PB, UK.

ISBN 978-1-84969-895-5

www.packtpub.com

Credits

Author

   Deepan Siddhu Nagarajan

Reviewer

   Navin Kumar Sivanesan

Acquisition Editors

   Pramila Balan

   Subho Gupta

Commissioning Editor

   Poonam Jain

Technical Editor

   Pankaj Kadam

Copy Editors

   Tanvi Gaitonde

   Dipti Kapadia

Project Coordinator

   Suraj Bist

Proofreader

   Paul Hindle

Production Coordinator

   Sushma Redkar

Cover Work

   Sushma Redkar

Cover Image

   Ronak Dhruv

About the Author

Deepan Siddhu Nagarajan is an engineer, marketer, and blogger who loves coffee. He works with Ripple Links as a Social Media Manager. As a marketer, he has worked with some of the world's largest brands and with several exciting startups in their most successful social media, SEO, SEM, content, and key influencer marketing campaigns. As an engineer, he has worked with India's largest telecommunication service providers and equipment manufacturers.

Deepan is also the founder of Digit-O-Metry, an online knowledge storehouse aimed at educating people with the best practices of modern marketing methodologies. Apart from being certified by renowned authorities such as HubSpot, Cambridge, IAMAI, NSE, and RAI in several educational disciplines, Deepan is also a featured contributor on top websites such as Business2Community, Memeburn, and Social Samosa. An avid reader, passionate blogger, public speaker, and a great listener, Deepan spends his leisure time blogging, training passionate students, and playing badminton.

He holds a postgraduate degree in Telecommunications and IT Management and an engineering degree in Electrical and Electronics from Anna University, Chennai.

I would like to thank my parents, Mr. Nagarajan and Mrs. Jegathy Mekala, my brothers, Mr. Surya Prakash Reddy and Mr. Raghu Ram Reddy, my dearest friend, Ms. Monica Krishna, and my best friends, Vijay Kannan, Saravaneswaran, Navin, and Sudharsan, who have always stood by and believed in me.

Special thanks go to Suraj and Poonam of Packt Publishing for giving me the opportunity to write a book on one of my most favorite subjects and Mr. Jeffrey Russo (Product Marketing Manager at HubSpot) for trusting me and giving me the go-ahead to write the book.

www.PacktPub.com

Support files, eBooks, discount offers and more

You might want to visit www.PacktPub.com for support files and downloads related to your book.

Did you know that Packt offers eBook versions of every book published, with PDF and ePub files available? You can upgrade to the eBook version at www.PacktPub.com and as a print book customer, you are entitled to a discount on the eBook copy. Get in touch with us at service@packtpub.com for more details.

At www.PacktPub.com, you can also read a collection of free technical articles, sign up for a range of free newsletters and receive exclusive discounts and offers on Packt books and eBooks.

http://PacktLib.PacktPub.com

Do you need instant solutions to your IT questions? PacktLib is Packt's online digital book library. Here, you can access, read and search across Packt's entire library of books.

Why Subscribe?

- ► Fully searchable across every book published by Packt
- ► Copy and paste, print and bookmark content
- ► On demand and accessible via web browser

Free Access for Packt account holders

If you have an account with Packt at www.PacktPub.com, you can use this to access PacktLib today and view nine entirely free books. Simply use your login credentials for immediate access.

—

Table of Contents

Preface   **1**

Instant HubSpot Dashboard Customization   **5**

Adding users to your account (Simple)   5
Connecting to HubSpot (Intermediate)   9
Setting up a social media and analytics tool (Intermediate)   11
Monitoring competition (Intermediate)   14
Managing e-mail marketing campaigns (Advanced)   17
Creating lead-nurturing campaigns (Advanced)   22
Tracking your campaign efforts (Intermediate)   25
Generating more traffic (Simple)   27
Becoming an SEO expert (Advanced)   31
Using the Link Grader tool (Intermediate)   35
Managing your social channels (Intermediate)   38
Using the social media publishing tool (Intermediate)   41
Using the social media prospects tool (Advanced)   44

Preface

Welcome to *Instant HubSpot Dashboard Customization*. This book will take you through the set of tasks that need to be performed to generate inbound leads for your business with the help of HubSpot.

What this book covers

Adding users to your account (Simple) will help you add multiple users to your HubSpot account. The HubSpot dashboard is extensive. It is really difficult for an individual to handle end-to-end activities if they're working for an organization running multiple marketing campaigns using HubSpot. Most companies set up additional user accounts and assign responsibilities accordingly in order to make the process easier.

Connecting to HubSpot (Intermediate) will show you how to connect your domain and subdomain to HubSpot. The step-by-step tasks will also help you connect the HubSpot-hosted landing page to your domain.

Setting up a social media and analytics tool (Intermediate) will help you integrate your multiple social media channels in one place using HubSpot along with a comprehensive dashboard to measure your analytics.

Monitoring competition (Intermediate) will show you how to closely monitor your competitors' website analytics and make appropriate changes to your website and marketing campaigns.

Managing e-mail marketing campaigns (Advanced) will help you create a killer e-mail marketing campaign with the strong call-to-action and social sharing functions in HubSpot.

Creating lead-nurturing campaigns (Advanced) will help you automate your e-mail marketing efforts based on the specific actions performed by a prospective client on your website.

Tracking your campaign efforts (Intermediate) will help you discern the effectiveness of different online marketing channels used for your campaign.

Generating more traffic (Simple) will show you how to use the different tools of HubSpot to generate content and optimize landing pages with the help of keyword searches and Search Engine Optimization (SEO) techniques.

Becoming an SEO expert (Advanced) consists of step-by-step procedures on how to apply SEO to your website so you can reap the benefits.

Using the Link Grader tool (Intermediate) will help you identify the inbound links of your competitors and show you how to optimize your link building activity.

Managing your social channels (Intermediate) will show you how to use different social media tools in HubSpot to drive traffic to your website or blog. Most people rely on search engines to drive traffic, but your social media channels, when optimized properly, can drive huge amounts of targeted traffic to your website or blog.

Using the social media publishing tool (Intermediate) will not only help you publish your blog posts to different channels, but also to understand the effectiveness of publishing your posts in each and every channel.

Using the social media prospects tool (Advanced) will help you monitor and engage with the conversations surrounding your brand and services, which will eventually help you generate more leads for your business and retain your existing customers.

What you need for this book

You should have a valid HubSpot account. This book is for anyone who wants to generate inbound leads for their business by customizing the HubSpot dashboard to their needs.

 HubSpot's GUI is updated regularly. The screenshots used in the chapter are those in accordance to the GUI at the time of writing the book. However, the recipes explained in the book are easily understandable and will work even on the latest version of HubSpot.

Conventions

In this book, you will find a number of styles of text that distinguish between different kinds of information. Here are some examples of these styles, and an explanation of their meaning.

Code words in text, database table names, folder names, filenames, file extensions, pathnames, dummy URLs, user input, and Twitter handles are shown as follows: "If you want the e-mail to be sent after a couple of days, set the option as 2 days, 0 hours, 0 minutes."

New terms and **important words** are shown in bold. Words that you see on the screen, in menus or dialog boxes for example, appear in the text like this: "Click on **Manage Users** located on the left-hand side of your browser."

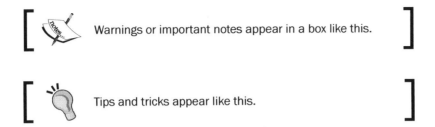

Warnings or important notes appear in a box like this.

Tips and tricks appear like this.

Reader feedback

Feedback from our readers is always welcome. Let us know what you think about this book—what you liked or may have disliked. Reader feedback is important for us to develop titles that you really get the most out of.

To send us general feedback, simply send an e-mail to feedback@packtpub.com, and mention the book title via the subject of your message.

If there is a topic that you have expertise in and you are interested in either writing or contributing to a book, see our author guide on www.packtpub.com/authors.

Customer support

Now that you are the proud owner of a Packt book, we have a number of things to help you to get the most from your purchase.

Errata

Although we have taken every care to ensure the accuracy of our content, mistakes do happen. If you find a mistake in one of our books—maybe a mistake in the text or the code—we would be grateful if you would report this to us. By doing so, you can save other readers from frustration and help us improve subsequent versions of this book. If you find any errata, please report them by visiting http://www.packtpub.com/submit-errata, selecting your book, clicking on the **errata submission form** link, and entering the details of your errata. Once your errata are verified, your submission will be accepted and the errata will be uploaded on our website, or added to any list of existing errata, under the Errata section of that title. Any existing errata can be viewed by selecting your title from http://www.packtpub.com/support.

Piracy

Piracy of copyright material on the Internet is an ongoing problem across all media. At Packt, we take the protection of our copyright and licenses very seriously. If you come across any illegal copies of our works, in any form, on the Internet, please provide us with the location address or website name immediately so that we can pursue a remedy.

Please contact us at `copyright@packtpub.com` with a link to the suspected pirated material.

We appreciate your help in protecting our authors, and our ability to bring you valuable content.

Questions

You can contact us at `questions@packtpub.com` if you are having a problem with any aspect of the book, and we will do our best to address it.

Instant HubSpot Dashboard Customization

Welcome to *Instant HubSpot Dashboard Customization*. HubSpot is a powerful all-in-one inbound marketing tool that helps a marketer to bring in more visitors to their website, convert visitors to leads, and transform those leads into sales.

This concise book will guide you through some of the customization features of HubSpot. It consists of easy, step-by-step procedures, from integrating your website with HubSpot to executing marketing campaigns and tracking the results. This book is ideal for anyone who wants to use HubSpot to help them attract more visitors to their website and convert them into leads.

Adding users to your account (Simple)

Why add users to a HubSpot account? If you are a premium user, HubSpot gives you the option of creating multiple logins for an account. This feature can be used by an individual to assign tasks to team members within or outside their organization depending on their requirements. Do take a look at the *How it works...* section of this recipe to understand more about the user roles. Let's take a look at how we can add users and assign roles to them.

Getting ready

As soon as you log in to your HubSpot account, you will get a pop up that asks you to provide your objectives. If you are a newbie, it's always better to start with **Attract more visitors**. Then, click on **Let's go**, as shown in the following screenshot:

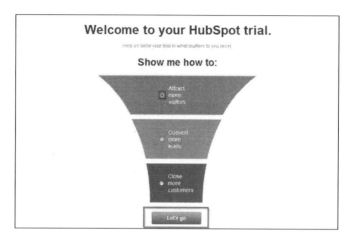

Next, you will be logged in to your account. Here, you will see five icons as shown in the following screenshot:

We will discuss these icons in the following recipes. Now, let's cover the basics that users need to know before they kick-start their optimization and marketing campaigns using HubSpot.

The HubSpot dashboard is extensive. It can be a challenge for a single individual to handle all of the end-to-end activities of an organization running multiple marketing campaigns. Most such companies set up additional user accounts and assign responsibilities accordingly to make the process easier.

How to do it...

The following is the step-by-step procedure to add users to your HubSpot account:

1. Click on your username located in the top-right corner of your account screen. Click on **Settings** from the drop-down menu as shown in the following screenshot:

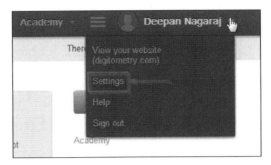

2. Click on **Manage Users**, located on the left-hand side of your browser:

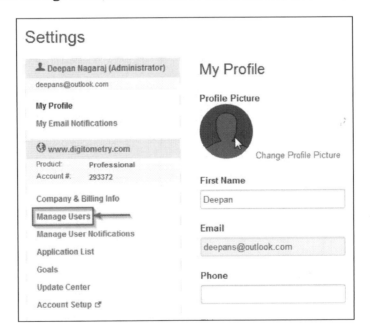

3. Click on the **Add User** button located in the top-right corner of your browser:

4. In the pop-up window, as shown in the following screenshot, enter information in the **Email**, **First Name**, **Last Name**, and **User Role** textboxes (refer to the table that immediately follows in the *How it works...* section of this recipe to read the detailed explanation), and then click on **Add User** at the bottom. Both you and the added user will be notified through e-mail at the completion of this process.

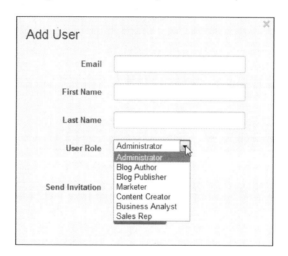

How it works...

The following table explains the different user roles:

User role	Access
Administrator	An administrator will have access to all the settings within your HubSpot account. This role is generally assigned to the owner of a website who has complete control over user management and domain settings.
Blog Author	A blog author can only create or modify the content of the blog app but not publish anything. This role is generally assigned to the content creators.
Blog Publisher	A blog publisher can create, modify, and publish the blog's content, but he/she will not have access to any other applications in the system.

User role	Access
Marketer	A marketer can access all the applications to perform core marketing tasks other than the settings for social media and analytics. This role is generally assigned to the marketing managers of an organization.
Content Creator	A content creator can access blogs, social media, keywords, call-to-actions, and other file manager applications. This role is generally assigned to the content creators who can create and promote content but don't need access to other technical aspects such as landing pages and workflows.
Business Analyst	A business analyst can access all the reporting tools in your HubSpot account. This role is generally assigned to professionals who deal with marketing metrics, intelligence, and creating reports.
Sales Rep	A sales rep can access the prospect's application but can only view the read-only version of any prospect's profile to which they've been assigned.

Connecting to HubSpot (Intermediate)

The objective of connecting a domain to HubSpot is very similar to the objective of an user to go for a HubSpot account which is to manage *many at one place*. A website plays a major role in being an identity for one's business and it should be given the utmost priority in terms of having quality content, adding additional pages for indexing, appropriate call-to-actions, and so on.

How to do it...

If you've created landing pages through your HubSpot account, here's how you can connect your domain name to your HubSpot-hosted landing page:

1. Go to your home page. Click on **Content** and then on **Content Settings** from the drop-down menu as shown in the following screenshot:

2. Click on **Domain Manager** under **Content Optimization System Tools** located on the left-hand side of your browser and then click on **Connect another HubSpot COS Domain** in the newly opened window. You will get a screen similar to the one shown in the following screenshot:

3. Enter the domain that you want to connect with HubSpot under the section **Your Domain**. You also have to provide HubSpot with your objective for connecting this domain. Is it only for landing pages? Or, is it for a blog or an entire website?

4. Click on the **Use for Content Publishing (email, landing pages)** option for landing pages, and click on **Use for Classic CMS (blog, full website pages)** if you want to connect your complete website. In case you are hosting your complete website through HubSpot, you will have to use a different subdomain name like we've used in the previous screenshot, **hub.digitometry.com**, where **hub** should be replaced with your subdomain name and **digitometry** should be replaced with your main domain name. Select one of the options according to your objective. If you want to connect the complete website, refer to the following screenshot:

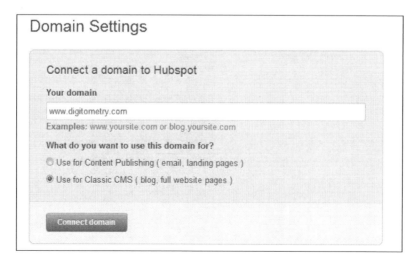

5. Once you have selected your option, click on **Connect domain**. You will get a screen similar to the following screenshot (if you've selected the **Use for Classic CMS** option in your previous step):

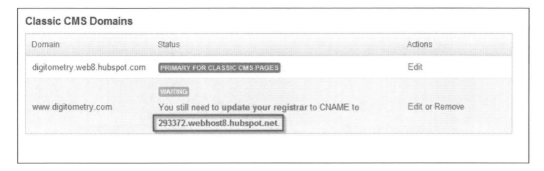

6. Copy the CNAME (the zone marked with red in the preceding screenshot).

7. If your domain is not hosted by HubSpot, you'll need to log in to your registrar and point the CNAME record to the one you've copied in the previous step. Now, get back to your HubSpot account and you will see the **WAITING** message removed from the **Status** column in somewhere between 30 minutes to 48 hours.

Setting up a social media and analytics tool (Intermediate)

Monitoring social media channels can prove cumbersome if the brand or company you're working for has its presence in multiple platforms. With this feature, HubSpot enables you to have complete control over your major social media channels in one place. Do read it completely to understand which social channels can be integrated into your HubSpot account.

Getting ready

Why should you integrate your social media channels with HubSpot? If you do this, all your blog posts can be automatically shared on your social channels. You'll also be able to view your social analytics through the Social Media Reach report.

How to do it...

1. Click on the **Social** tab and then select **Social Settings** as shown in the following screenshot:

2. You will see plugins for popular social networks. Select a plugin based on your requirements by clicking on its appropriate button (for example, if you want to connect your Facebook page, click on **Add Facebook account**). As of the time of writing, you can connect a maximum of seven social media accounts. HubSpot might roll out other social network plugins soon.

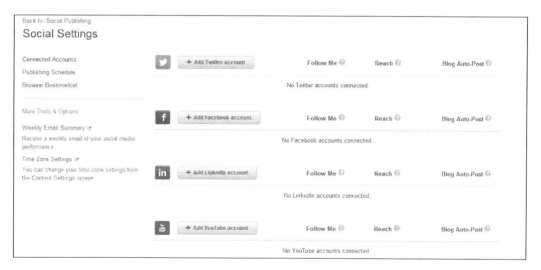

3. Let's add a Facebook page to make it clear. When you click on **Add Facebook account**, a response screen will prompt you to authorize your account on Facebook. Click on the call-to-action and you will be taken to the Facebook login page:

4. After logging in to your Facebook account, HubSpot will ask you to grant access to information such as friends and contact info, websites, descriptions, and others.

5. Next, HubSpot will ask for permission to post publicly on your behalf, and you can either choose the option **Okay** or **Skip**. Most prefer clicking on the **Skip** button when providing access to third-party applications, as people don't want anything posted on their page or profile without prior notice.

6. The next step in this process is that HubSpot will request for your permission to manage your pages. Click on **Okay** during this step as shown in the following screenshot:

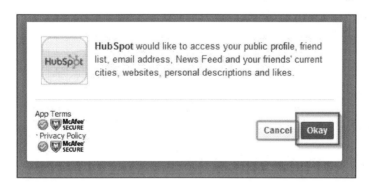

7. Once you complete the process, you will be taken back to your HubSpot account where you can see the pages you manage (with your Facebook account). Select the **Follow Me**, **Reach**, and **Blog Auto-Post** options only for the pages you want to integrate with Facebook:

Monitoring competition (Intermediate)

We all need to know what our competitors are up to. With the HubSpot competitor monitoring tool, you can quickly and easily monitor your competitors' activities.

How to do it...

Monitoring competition is not just an activity to check what your competitors are upto but to spot positive or negative remarks around them, in order to improve your business operations or to collect information needed to plan your promotional activities and so on. The following steps will guide you to monitor your competition with the HubSpot competitor monitoring tool:

1. Click on the **Reports** tab and select **Competitors** as shown in the following screenshot:

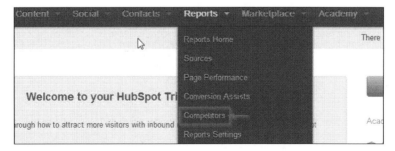

2. Click on **Add New Competitor**, enter the website URL of your competitor, and click on **Add**:

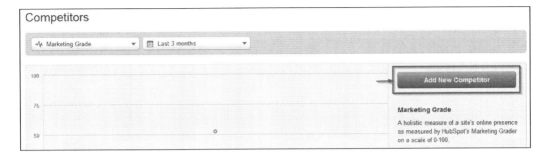

3. Perform step 2 again to add more competitors. After the completion of this process, you will find your competitors listed in the chart at the bottom of the **Competitors** page (right below the graph):

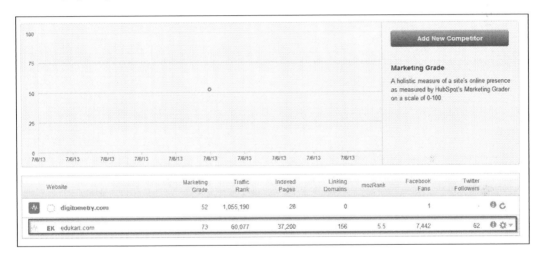

4. Click on the graph icon that is placed before the name of your competitors to view their activity on the graph. You can try changing the metrics (such as **Traffic Rank, Indexed Pages, Facebook Fans**, and **mozRank**) in the first filter and the date range in the second filter (**Last 30 days, Last 3 months**, and so on):

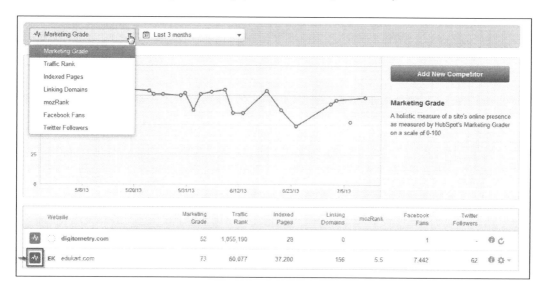

5. You can also hover over the dots in the graph to get detailed information of the changes as shown in the following screenshot:

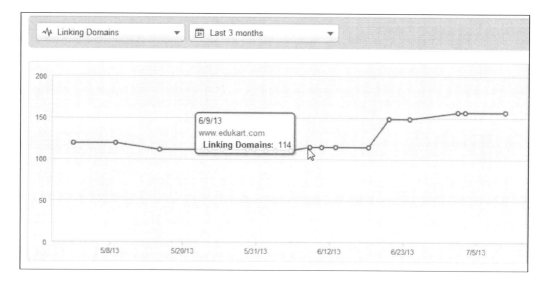

Managing e-mail marketing campaigns (Advanced)

An e-mail marketing campaign is not just about the click-through rates. These days, the majority of brands buy consumer lists and send annoying e-mails to their prospects. HubSpot provides you with a more effective way of automating your e-mail marketing campaigns, based on actions taken by your prospects, in order to build a strong and engaged pipeline. Let's take a look at how you can go about it.

Getting ready

A great feature that HubSpot provides is the ability to create and automate all your e-mail marketing and lead-nurturing campaigns with the help of the Workflows tool. Based on the action completed by your lead on your website, an automated e-mail with an appropriate call-to-action will be sent to him/her. Though you can create *n* number of workflows with your HubSpot account, take a look at the following example to understand how a workflow can be created.

How to do it...

1. Create an e-mail through HubSpot. Select the **Email** option from the **Content** tab as shown in the following screenshot:

2. If you want to configure a logo for your e-mails, click on **Set up HubSpot Content Tools** and follow the instructions. If not, click on the **Set up email** option next to it as shown in the following screenshot:

3. Next, upload your logo and click on **Save Logo**:

4. Next, choose the fonts and colors and click on **Save**.

5. In the next step, you will have to fill in the sender's information such as company name and address (U.S. and international laws require that all e-mails should have sender information) and then click on **Save CAN-SPAM Information**.

6. Next, click on the **Create email** option as shown in the following screenshot:

7. Follow the simple instructions provided and design your e-mail according to your requirements. Give it a name, select a template, and then click on **Create Email**. You can also check the preview of the e-mail on the right-hand side of the browser. Have a look at the following screenshot:

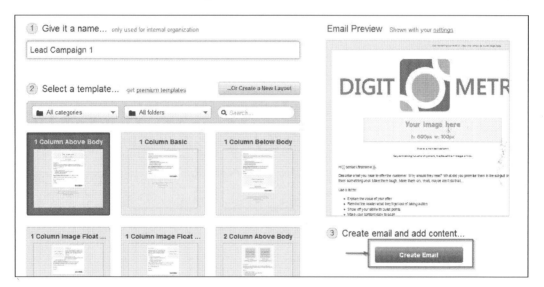

8. Now is the important step of deciding how your final e-mail (to be sent to your leads) will look. Fill out all the basic information such as the sender name and e-mail address, name of the campaign, subject of the message, and content of the e-mail body. If you want to personalize the sender details, click on the **Personalize Sender** option and select one of the options (based on how you want to personalize the details).

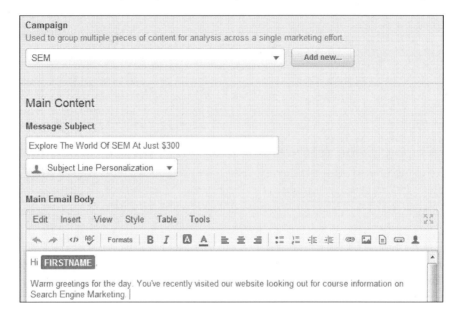

9. If you want to give the recipients an option of sharing a particular link on their social media profiles, make sure you turn on the relevant social media buttons under **Social Sharing**. The link could be your landing pages or your social media profiles. For example, we've given a sample Facebook page here:

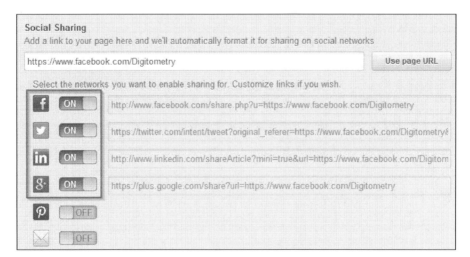

10. Once you are done with how your e-mail should look, it's time to create a text-ready version. (This is for users with slow Internet connection who cannot open an HTML copy on a mobile device.) Click on **Options** in your **Email** dashboard and type the text version of your e-mail in the box titled **Customize Plain Text Version** as shown in the following screenshot:

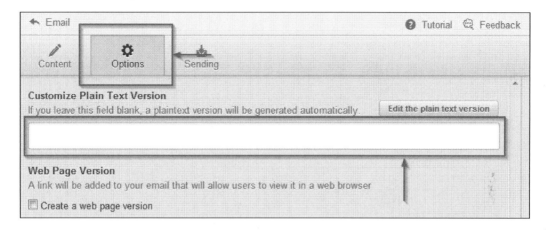

11. Once you are done with defining all the other settings and design of the HTML and text versions of your e-mail, it's time to send your e-mail. Select the **Sending** option in your **Email** dashboard and you will be able to see three other options. You can send your e-mails immediately, at a scheduled date and time, or with automated workflows (this will be discussed in detail in the upcoming recipes):

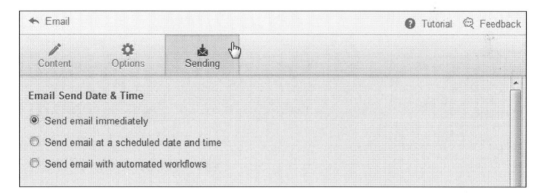

Creating lead-nurturing campaigns (Advanced)

"One size fits all" is an approach that should never be followed if you want to generate qualified leads for your business. If you want to generate decent responses to your e-mail campaign, you will have to follow the approach of sending highly targeted e-mails to your prospects. If you can automate this process, it's going to save you a lot of time.

Getting ready

As we discussed earlier, we should use the Workflows tool for lead-nurturing campaigns. With this tool, you can create a lead-nurturing campaign to generate leads, convert warm leads to hot leads, send an automated response through e-mail when a visitor fills a form on your website, and also segment the leads based on their actions.

How to do it...

1. In order to create a workflow, we need to follow the set of instructions given in the previous recipe, *Managing e-mail marketing campaigns*, to create an e-mail (the HTML and text versions). In the **Email** dashboard, click on the **Sending** tab, select the **Send email with automated workflows** option, and then click on **Save**, as shown in the following screenshot:

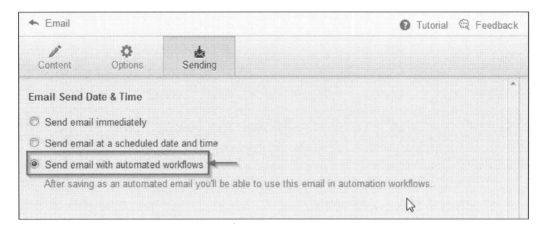

2. In the **Contacts** tab, click on **Workflows** as shown in the following screenshot:

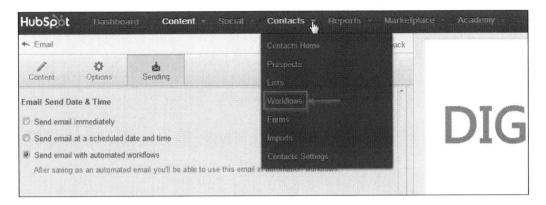

3. As shown in the following screenshot, click on the **Create new workflow** button and give your workflow a name:

4. Select a condition for your workflow, a form (landing page), and the page on which you want the workflow based on your requirements, as shown in the following screenshot:

5. On the same page, right below the workflow activations, you will also have to define the workflow steps (how you want the workflow to happen). If you want an e-mail to be immediately sent to your prospect right after they fill in a form on your website, you might have to set the **Delay this step for** option to 0 days, 0 hours, and 0 minutes, and then select the action **Send an email** (the different options are discussed in detail in the table in the *How it works...* section of this recipe). If you want the e-mail to be sent after a couple of days, set the option to 2 days, 0 hours, and 0 minutes. Click on **Save Workflow** to ensure the completion of this process.

How it works...

The following table will explain the different options and their actions in creating workflows:

Workflow options	Functions
Send an email	Send an e-mail to a contact based on their actions.
Set a contact property value	Assign a value to your contact for further actions to be taken.
Add to/Remove from a list	Segment your contacts under different buckets based on actions.
Increment a numeric property value	Add or subtract the value based on contact's position in the workflow.
Copy a contact property value	Copy a contact's property value to another contact based on the actions.
Trigger a webhook	This includes a wide range of options, such as triggering offers, sending SMS alerts, Facebook posting, following up, and so on.
Send internal email	This option will trigger an e-mail to your internal team for the appropriate actions to be taken.
Send an internal SMS	This option will trigger a text message to your internal team for the appropriate actions to be taken.

Tracking your campaign efforts (Intermediate)

Why is tracking so important? It helps us understand what has been successful, what hasn't, and the areas of improvement for a campaign. It also helps us understand the impact of different online marketing initiatives. The metrics will change from one campaign to another depending on the goals for each.

Getting ready

To measure the effectiveness of your marketing campaigns, you will have to use tracking URLs. Tracking URLs help us understand the different sources of traffic for our website (they might include organic, **Pay Per Click** (**PPC**), social media, e-mail, and so on). Let's go ahead and learn how to create a tracking URL for our landing pages.

How to do it...

1. In the **Reports** tab, click on **Reports Home** as shown in the following screenshot:

2. Click on **Tracking URL Builder** to the right-hand side of the page and then click on **Create New Tracking URL** on the next page. If you're running an e-mail marketing campaign through HubSpot, you don't have to do this, as HubSpot, by default, does this for you.

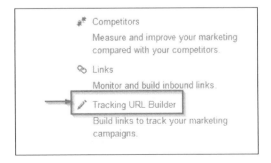

3. Fill in all the information, such as the URL (the one you want to track), campaign name, campaign sources (the different places where you will be using this link; for example, PPC, e-mail, social media, and so on), and marketing actions (internal use); then, click on **Generate** as shown in the following screenshot:

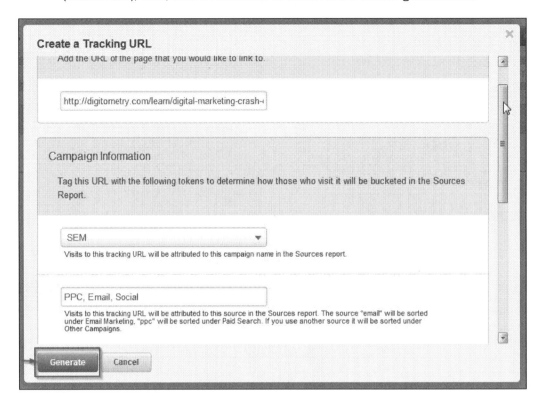

4. You will get a new window with the original link and the tracking URL. You can copy the shortened URL from there or access it under the **Tracking URLs** page. Use this URL in all your e-marketing channels, such as Google AdWords, Bing Ads, social media, e-mails, and so on.

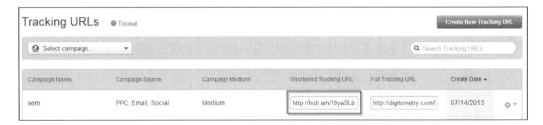

5. To measure the results, click on **Sources** in the **Reports** tab and click on **Other Campaigns** to see how your tracking URLs are performing. You can also check the sources by scrolling down on the page.

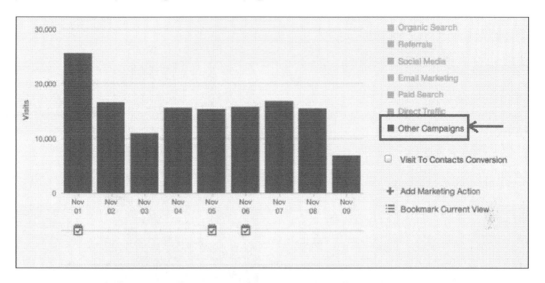

Generating more traffic (Simple)

Now it's time to do some inbound marketing. A company cannot rely on just its outbound marketing efforts in the long run. Key techniques and methodologies, such as SEO, whitepapers, and blogs, can create a lot of brand visibility and help the business in generating a huge number of qualified leads.

Getting ready

This section will show you how to use the different tools of HubSpot to generate content and optimize landing pages with the help of keyword searches and SEO techniques.

How to do it...

1. Click on **Content** and then select **Keywords** from the drop-down menu as shown in the following screenshot:

2. Click on **Add Keywords** as shown in the following screenshot:

3. Add two or three relevant keywords for your business in the textbox named **Add new keywords (one per line)** and then select the campaign to which you want to add the keywords. You can also click on **Get suggestions** (in case you don't have a set of keywords for your business) as shown in the following screenshot:

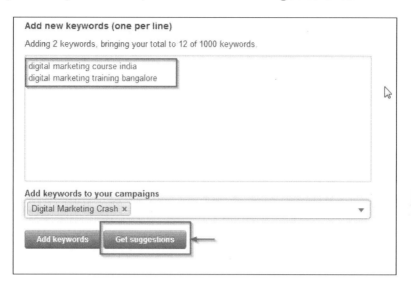

4. Type business-relevant keywords in the search box and HubSpot will churn out a number of relevant keywords with a number of search results. The following screenshot shows what the **Keyword Suggestions** window will look like:

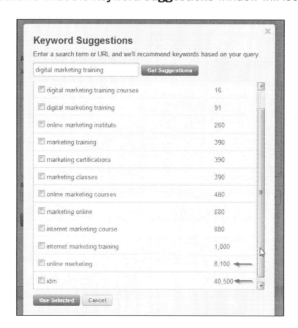

5. It's advisable to select keywords with a high number of searches. In the previous example, the keywords **online marketing** and **idm** have a considerably higher number of searches compared to all the other keywords. However, it is also important to select the most relevant keywords. In the example, the keyword **online marketing** makes sense for a company which is into digital marketing training, whereas the keyword **idm** does not. Filter the appropriate keywords for your business in this step. Once you finalize which keywords to select, check the checkboxes for those keywords and click on the **Use Selected** button as shown in the following screenshot:

6. Now all the selected keywords that we were discussing in step 5 will be added to the **Add new keywords (one per line)** textbox. Click on **Add keywords** to finish the process, as shown in the following screenshot:

7. You can also go back to the **Keywords** page to check how the keywords in different campaigns are performing as shown in the following screenshot:

Becoming an SEO expert (Advanced)

The objective of applying SEO to a website is to make it easy for search engines and users to understand what your website (or web page) is all about. It plays a very important role in users' buying cycle, depending upon the position of your web pages in Google search results for targeted keywords. You need not be an expert to apply basic tweaks to your SEO efforts when HubSpot is there to guide you through it.

Getting ready

Now that you've understood how to pick up relevant keywords for your business, it's time to incorporate those keywords in certain places on your web page to make it easier for Google and other search engines to rank your page accordingly. Do not confuse the search engines by using many different keywords in your page rather than one specific primary keyword.

How to do it...

1. To apply SEO, navigate to one of the pages you've created through HubSpot. In the **Content** tab, select **Page Manager** from the drop-down menu as shown in the following screenshot:

2. Right-click on one of the pages (to which you want to apply SEO) and select **Page Properties** as shown in the following screenshot:

3. Your page title must have your primary keyword (that must be relevant to your page and business), which should not be longer than 70 characters. You may also have your brand name in the page title, and it will appear on Google SERPs as underlined text. Make sure you don't repeat the page titles for any of your pages, as it might result in confusing Google to present your page in front of the user searching for a particular keyword.

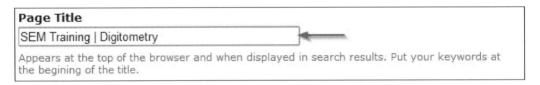

4. The next thing to check is your page URL. Make sure the URL has your primary keyword. For example, the primary keyword for the sample page we used in the following screenshot is **SEM Training**; we've used it along with the region's name:

5. Another major SEO element of any page is its meta description. A meta description of your page appears right below your page title in the Google search results. Make sure that your meta description contains the primary keyword of your page

6. and that it is no longer than 150 characters. Avoid using multiple keywords and try to form a meaningful description in the **Meta Description** section. The following screenshot shows the **Meta Description** section:

7. Meta keywords were considered by Google to rank your pages a long time ago. Though it's not very important when your focus is on Google and Yahoo, it's good to keep them optimized for smaller search engines to find you. The following screenshot will give you an idea of how to write meta keywords:

8. Once you are done with the basic SEO elements of your page, it's time to optimize your content. Make sure your primary keyword appears a few times in your page content. You can also make the text stand out from the rest by making it bold. For example, in the following screenshot, we can make the text **SEM Training Course** bold:

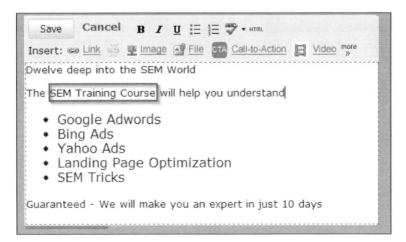

9. Use anchor text in all the links that you use in the content of your page. The anchor text will help Google understand what the link is all about. In the following screenshot, the anchor text is **SEM Training Course,** and the link will lead to the **SEM Training Course Details** page on the website. To add a link, select the text and click on **Link**. Insert an internal/external link accordingly.

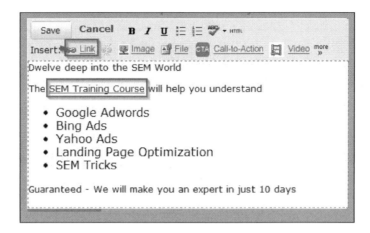

10. If you have an image in your content, you have to let Google know what it is. This can be done by changing the filename and **alt text** of the image. If you want to change the alt text of the image, click on **Image** in the tool bar, search for alt text using the search box to the right-hand side of the window, and change the name accordingly. You can also include your primary keyword here if the image is relevant to your business, page content, and the other basic SEO elements.

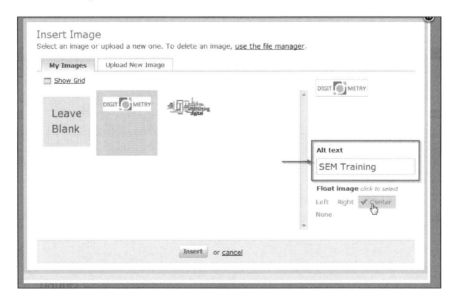

Using the Link Grader tool (Intermediate)

Building quality links for your website is one of the most important activities of SEO. It is the process that involves working with other websites to use links in appropriate places (that are relevant to your business) to bring in traffic for your website.

Getting ready

HubSpot's Link Grader tool lets you know of your own inbound links and also those of your competitors.

How to do it...

1. In the **Reports** tab, select **Page Performance** from the drop-down menu as shown in the following screenshot:

2. Click on **Links** to the right-hand side of your browser:

3. Select a competitor from the drop-down list and see the number of inbound links to your competitor's website. You can prepare a list and target the same websites to build quality inbound links for your website.

4. With the Link Grader tool, you can check the inbound links for any domain by clicking on the **Find links for any domain** option as shown in the following screenshot:

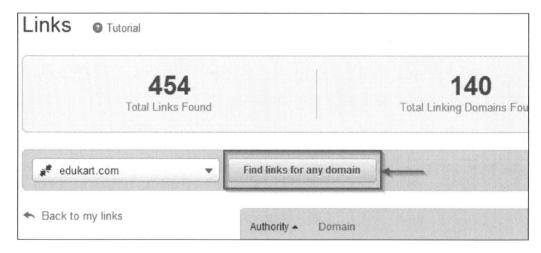

5. Enter the domain name in the **Domain** textbox and click on **Find** as shown in the following screenshot:

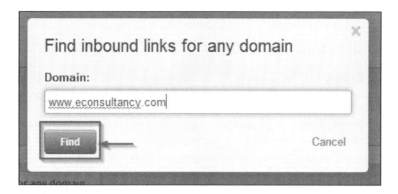

6. Now you will be able to see the websites linking back to the domain you just entered. Not all the inbound links are good. HubSpot also helps you with the **authority rank** to determine the quality of the inbound link. The authority rank is based on the online reputation of that website specifically. Make sure you target the websites with a decent authority rank and start building inbound links.

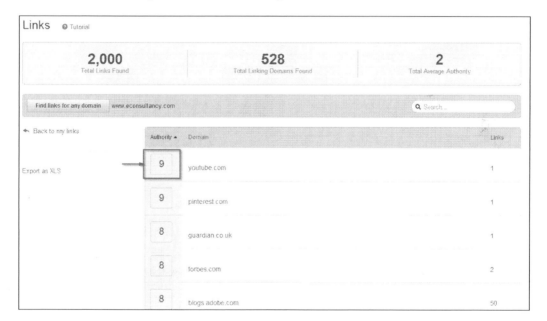

Managing your social channels (Intermediate)

Targeted traffic is the lifeline of any website or blog. Most people rely on search engines for their traffic; but, when your social media channels are optimized properly, they can drive a huge amount of targeted traffic to your website or blog. This section will show you how to use the different social media tools provided by HubSpot to drive traffic to your website or blog.

Getting ready

Blogs came way before Facebook, Twitter, and Google+, and they're still going strong. Every time you blog, you get a chance to get another one of your pages indexed by Google. Let's have a look at how we can use the Blog tool provided by HubSpot.

How to do it...

1. Refer to the *Generating more traffic* recipe to identify keywords by difficulty and competition level. Make sure the title of your blog contains the relevant keywords.

   Now, in the **Content** tab, select **Blog** from the drop-down list as shown in the following screenshot:

2. Now, select the **Create Article** option, which is located right under the **Using the HubSpot Blog** section, as shown in the following screenshot:

3. If you look at the right-hand side of your browser now, HubSpot will be trying to help you out by displaying the important elements that are missing from the blog. Start filling in all those elements one-by-one.

4. Enter your keyword-rich blog title in the textbox named **Title** and your content in the text area named **Article Body**. A blog should contain no fewer than 500 words. Use the options **Bold**, **Italic**, and **Underline** whenever required. Avoid writing a full-length essay. Try to use subheadings, numbers, and bullets.

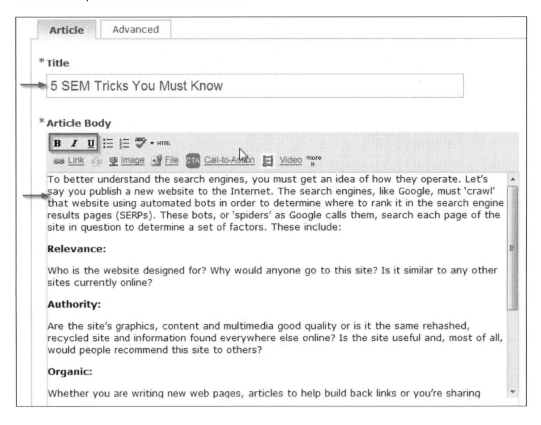

5. An image can speak a thousand words. Make sure you insert a relevant image for your blog, as images have the ability to drive decent traffic to your blog or website. Don't forget to give a relevant name and alt text attribute for the image you attach along with the keywords you identified. You can also select the option **Left**, **Right**, or **Center** depending upon where you want the image to be displayed in your blog.

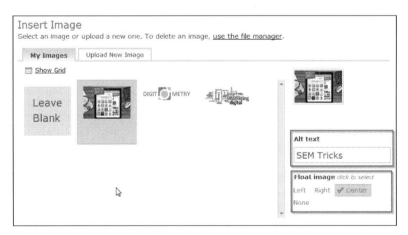

6. Make sure the tags you add are relevant to the blog. Tags are generally used in a blog to make it easier for the reader to identify the topic they are looking for. Once you are done with the tags, click on the **Publish** button to make your blog go live as shown in the following screenshot:

Using the social media publishing tool (Intermediate)

Now that you've created your first blog post, it's time to figure out how to market it. With HubSpot's social media publishing tool, you can promote your content on different social channels as well as post an update to all your social channels at once. You can also track the effectiveness of a particular post on different social channels.

How to do it...

The essence of social media success lies in trying out new methods, monitoring the performance for few days, and then taking a call on which method to go for, in a long run. Now let's understand how do we achieve it using HubSpot. The following steps will guide you to use the HubSpot's social media publishing tool:

1. Refer to the *Setting up a social media and analytics tool* recipe to learn how to integrate all your social media accounts with HubSpot.

2. Once you are done with step 1, in the **Social** tab, click on **Publishing** from the drop-down list as shown in the following screenshot:

3. Click on the **Compose a message** option located to the right-hand side of your browser as shown in the following screenshot:

4. In the message box, type the message (the one you want to publish on any of your social media channels). You can also attach a blog post, landing page, or image by clicking on the options located just above the message box as shown in the following screenshot:

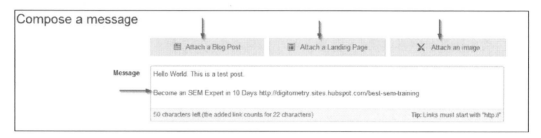

5. The next step is to select the social media accounts on which you want to publish the message. You can post it on your Twitter account, personal Facebook account, Facebook pages (to which you have admin access), personal LinkedIn profiles, LinkedIn company profiles (to which you have admin access), and LinkedIn groups (to which you have membership access) as shown in the following screenshot:

6. If you want your post to be published immediately, you don't have to change any settings here on this page. If you want to schedule its publishing to a later time, click on **Add Additional Time** and select the appropriate date and time for your post, as shown in the following screenshot:

7. The next step is to select one of your campaigns in order to track the effectiveness of your campaign-related posts on different social media channels. Once you are done, click on the **Schedule All** option as shown in the following screenshot:

8. Now you will be able to see the list of scheduled posts and the social channels which have been assigned. In case you want to make any changes or delete the post or a schedule, click on the **Settings** icon located to the right-hand side of your posts and select the desired option:

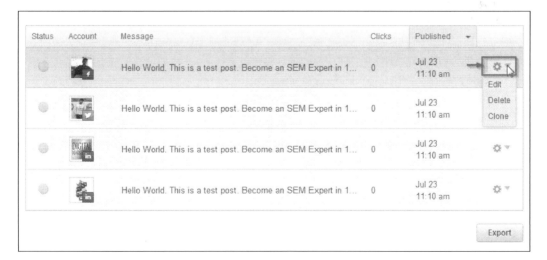

9. If you want to track the effectiveness of your posts on different social media channels, look out for the **Clicks** column right next to your scheduled posts. The number of clicks received shows the effectiveness of your posts on different social media channels. If you want to monitor the effectiveness of a channel, click on the box that shows **All Channels** and select a channel.

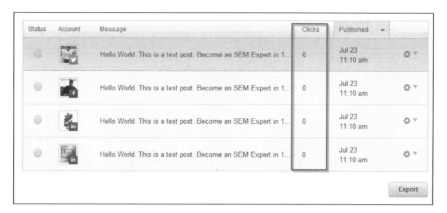

Using the social media prospects tool (Advanced)

Using social media has multiple benefits. It ends up not only promoting your blog posts and offers, but also helps you in building relationships with your existing and target customers, industry influencers, and so on. Monitoring and engaging with the conversations surrounding your brand, product, and service are two of the most important social media activities that a brand should perform. Let's explore how the social media prospects tool provided by HubSpot helps us achieve this.

How to do it...

The objective is not just to engage with positive conversations around your brand but also around the negative conversations which will have a deep impact on your business. One can also use this option to discover influencers talking about their brand/industry, to monitor the competition, to spot the crisis or to manage a crisis. The following steps will guide you to use the HubSpot's social media prospects tool:

1. In the **Content** tab, select **Social Media** from the drop-down list as shown in the following screenshot:

2. Click on the **Monitoring** option, which is located to the right-hand side of your browser, as shown in the following screenshot:

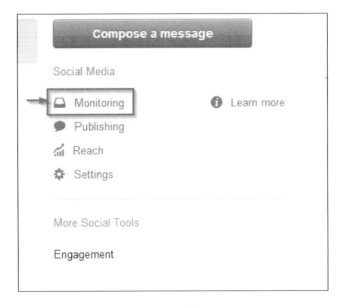

3. Now, with the **Social Inbox** screen in front of you, click on the **Get started with Social Inbox** button as shown in the following screenshot:

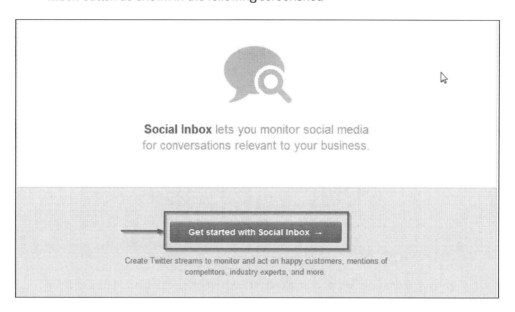

4. You will have to connect your Twitter account (personal/business) depending on your requirement for monitoring. You can also connect a different Twitter account by selecting the **Connect another Twitter account** option. Once you are done selecting your account for monitoring, click on the **Enable monitoring for these accounts** option as shown in the following screenshot:

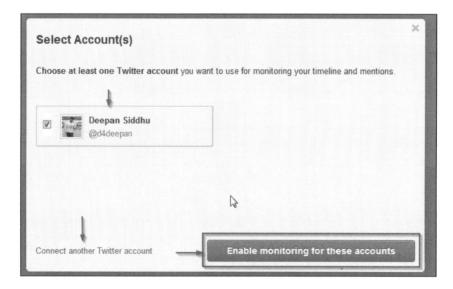

5. You will see a screen with the message **All done**, which means your account is successfully connected to monitor the tweets and mentions, as shown in the following screenshot:

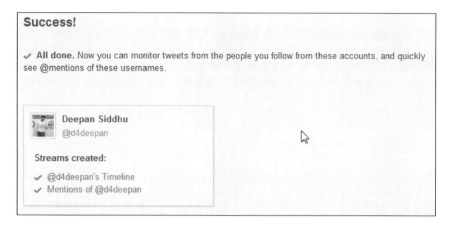

6. It's time to monitor for your business-relevant keywords and start engaging with them. You have the options for monitoring all of Twitter, a Twitter list, or a contact list. In the following example, we've selected the **All of Twitter** option and specified a few business-relevant keywords under the column **Find ANY of these words** to look out for relevant conversations. You can also specify an e-mail ID under the **Notify these recipients** column to get real-time alerts straight to your inbox. Based on the keywords you track, assign a name for the stream to avoid confusion. Once you are done with the basic settings, click on the **Create** button to ensure the completion of the process of creating a stream to monitor, as shown in the following screenshot:

7. Now you will be able to see the relevant Twitter conversations surrounding your business right on your screen, similar to the following screenshot. Pick up the most relevant tweets and start engaging with them. If it's an industry influencer mentioning your name, you could retweet them or reply, thanking them. If it's a business opportunity, try to give appropriate information or guide the user to your landing page where they can find relevant information. Make sure that you don't retweet or reply to any of your competitors' tweets.

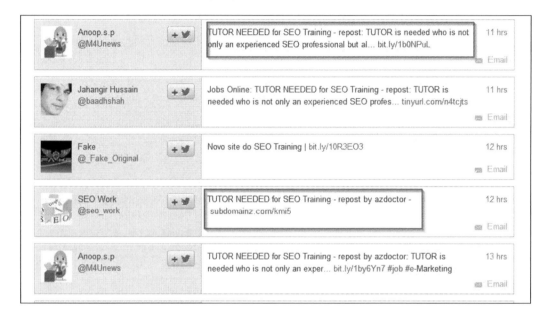

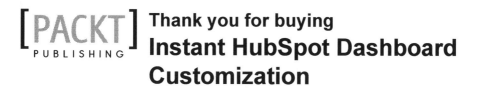

Thank you for buying
Instant HubSpot Dashboard Customization

About Packt Publishing

Packt, pronounced 'packed', published its first book "*Mastering phpMyAdmin for Effective MySQL Management*" in April 2004 and subsequently continued to specialize in publishing highly focused books on specific technologies and solutions.

Our books and publications share the experiences of your fellow IT professionals in adapting and customizing today's systems, applications, and frameworks. Our solution based books give you the knowledge and power to customize the software and technologies you're using to get the job done. Packt books are more specific and less general than the IT books you have seen in the past. Our unique business model allows us to bring you more focused information, giving you more of what you need to know, and less of what you don't.

Packt is a modern, yet unique publishing company, which focuses on producing quality, cutting-edge books for communities of developers, administrators, and newbies alike. For more information, please visit our website: www.packtpub.com.

Writing for Packt

We welcome all inquiries from people who are interested in authoring. Book proposals should be sent to author@packtpub.com. If your book idea is still at an early stage and you would like to discuss it first before writing a formal book proposal, contact us; one of our commissioning editors will get in touch with you.

We're not just looking for published authors; if you have strong technical skills but no writing experience, our experienced editors can help you develop a writing career, or simply get some additional reward for your expertise.

Internet Marketing with WordPress

ISBN: 978-1-84951-674-7   Paperback: 112 pages

Use the power of WordPress to target customers, increase traffic, and build your business

1. Get practical experience in key aspects of online marketing

2. Accurately identify your business objectives and target audience to maximize your marketing efficiency

3. Create and deliver awesome SEO-enhanced, targeted content to drive large numbers of visitors through your blog

Social Media for WordPress Beginner's Guide

ISBN: 978-1-84719-980-5   Paperback: 166 pages

A quicker way to build communities, engage members, and promote your site

1. Integrate automated key marketing techniques

2. Examine analytical data to measure social engagement

3. Understand the core principles of establishing meaningful social connections

Please check **www.PacktPub.com** for information on our titles

Drupal 7 Social Networking

ISBN: 978-1-84951-600-6   Paperback: 328 pages

Build a social or community website with friends lists, groups, customer user profiles, and much more

1. Step-by-step instructions for putting together a social networking site with Drupal 7

2. Customize your Drupal installation with modules and themes to match the needs of almost any social networking site

3. Allow users to collaborate and interact with each other on your site

4. Requires no prior knowledge of Drupal or PHP; but even experienced Drupal users will find this book useful to modify an existing installation into a social website

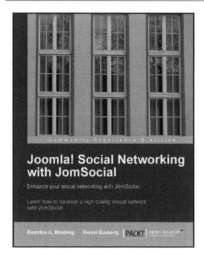

Joomla! Social Networking with JomSocial

ISBN: 978-1-84719-956-0   Paperback: 184 pages

Learn how to develop a high quality social network with JomSocial

1. Create and run your own social network with Joomla! and JomSocial

2. Creating content for the social network and integrating it with other Joomla! extensions

3. Community building and interactions

Please check **www.PacktPub.com** for information on our titles

Made in the USA
San Bernardino, CA
01 November 2018